Presented to

_____

from

_____

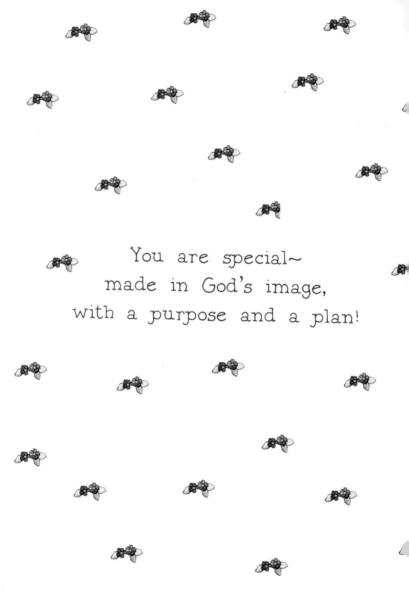

You are special~
made in God's image,
with a purpose and a plan!

I Celebrate You!

Karla Dornacher

COUNTRYMAN

Thank you for giving
so much to me,

a treasured friend
you will always be.

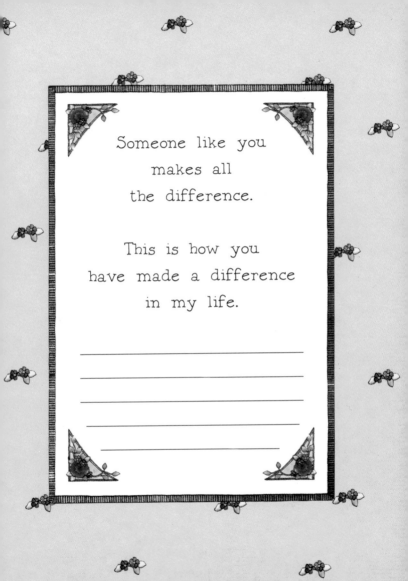

Someone like you
makes all
the difference.

This is how you
have made a difference
in my life.

_____

_____

_____

_____

_____

You deserve a hug...

just because
you're you!

(The world is a better place

because you are in it.)

You bring happiness to others by

_____

_____

_____

_____

_____

_____

_____

_____

_____

_____

_____

_____

You're the kind of person
I'm glad I know!

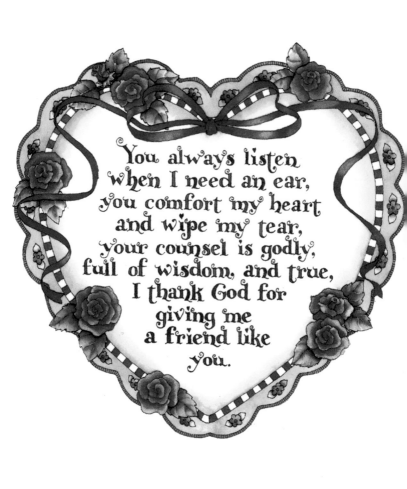

You always listen
when I need an ear,
you comfort my heart
and wipe my tear,
your counsel is godly,
full of wisdom, and true,
I thank God for
giving me
a friend like
you.

How many times
you have shown me,
what a wonderful
heart you
have!

Rejoice with those who rejoice

Life is a song. Sing it.
Life is love. Enjoy it.

~Mother Teresa

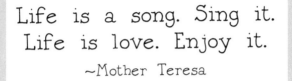

You inspire me to

_____

_____

_____

_____

_____

_____

Some flowers that grow in the garden of life:

Goldenrod	cautious
Gladiolus	strong in character
Heather	beauty in solitude
Scarlet geranium	comforting
White daisy	innocence
Coreopsis	always cheerful
Columbine	steadfast
Alyssum	sweetness of soul
Red Poppy	consolation
Scarlet Poppy	extravagance
Peony	bashful
Pansy	happy thoughts
Mimosa	sensitive

Faithfully tend the
flowers in the garden
of your life.

Little acts of kindness are like flowers by life's wayside ~ Anonymous

BLOOM·WHERE·YOU'RE·PLANTED·

I'm so thankful that
God planted you
in my life.

You have added a
beauty and sweet
fragrance like no
other ever could.

These are some of the quality character traits I appreciate in you:

_____

_____

_____

_____

_____

_____

I'd like to be the sort of friend that you have been to me.

~Edgar H. Guest

Keep your face to the sunshine and you cannot see the shadows.

Helen Keller

For you, I pray~
freedom to dream big dreams,
encouragement to reach
for the stars,
faith in the One who makes
all things possible,
and courage to be uniquely
who you are.

May the sunshine
of God's love
warm your heart
and
brighten your day.

With friends we
plant the seeds of our heart's
new dreams.

~Susan Florence

You
are
one
of a
kind.

Cherish
what
makes
you
unique.

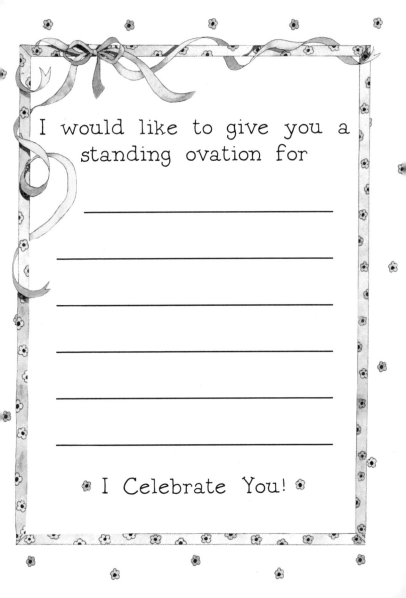

I would like to give you a
standing ovation for

_____

_____

_____

_____

_____

_____

❀ I Celebrate You! ❀